LEARN-TO-READ
TREASURE HUNTS

---

50 SKILL-BUILDING GAMES FOR BEGINNING READERS AND THEIR PARENTS

STEVE COHEN
(WITH HELP FROM HIS SON PETER, AGE 10)

ILLUSTRATED BY SCOT RITCHIE

Workman Publishing • New York

Workman books are available at special discount when purchased in bulk for special premiums and sales promotions as well as for fund-raising or educational use. Special editions or book excerpts also can be created to specification. For details, contact the Special Sales Director at the address below.

Workman Publishing Company, Inc.
708 Broadway
New York, NY 10003-9555

Manufactured in the United States of America

First Printing March 1997
10 9 8 7 6 5 4 3 2 1

Good morning
Today is a treasure hunt day. There are 3 clues.

1. Where do you keep your pajamas? (Some people call them PJ's.) Look there.

Put this where you'd like today's hunt to begin.

2. Look behind the roll of toilet paper in the bathroom.

*Put this where you keep
your child's pajamas.*

3. **Where do you keep your shoes? Look in one of your left shoes.**

*Put this in the bathroom
behind the toilet paper.*

Super! Come get your sticker.

★ BONUS GAME
MATCH IT!

spy

knight

bubble

hanger

light switch

Put this in one of your child's left shoes.

Hello
Today is a treasure hunt
day. There are four clues.

1. Open the refrigerator door and take a look inside.

Put this where you'd like today's hunt to begin.

2. Look on the floor behind the chair near the TV.

Put this inside the refrigerator.

3. Where do I sleep? Look under the blanket.

*Put this on the floor behind
the chair near the TV.*

4. Look in the place where we keep your socks.

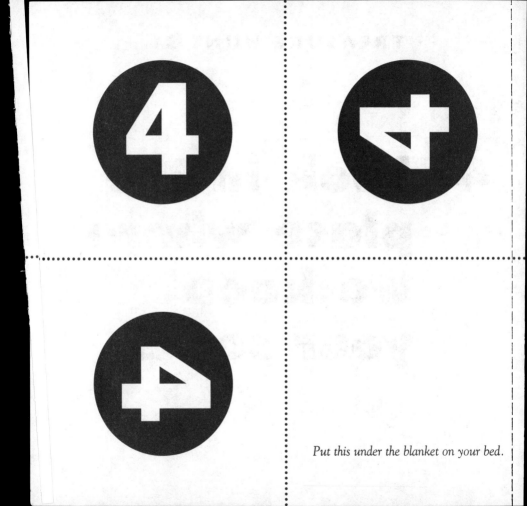

Put this under the blanket on your bed.

Fantastic! Come get your sticker.

MATCH IT!

BONUS GAME

flame

flag

flashlight

flower

floor

Hello again
Today is a treasure hunt
day. There are four clues.

**1. Open the
newspaper to
page 3. You
will find the
next clue there.**

Put this where you'd like today's hunt to begin.

2. Do you know where we keep cheese?

Put this on page 3 of the newspaper.

3. When you want to sleep, you put your head on something soft. Look under it.

Put this where you keep cheese.

4. Look in the drawer where we keep your socks.

Put this under your child's pillow.

Well done! Come get your sticker.

MATCH IT!

cheese

trees

squeeze

knees

bees

Put this in your child's sock drawer.

Good morning
Today is a treasure hunt
day. There are four clues.

**1. Try a place
close to your
toothbrush.**

Put this where you'd like today's hunt to begin.

2. **In your closet, take a look in a right shoe.**

Put this close to your child's toothbrush.

3. Check on the kitchen floor near the place where we keep pots and pans.

Put this in one of your child's right shoes in his or her closet.

4. Is there a clock in your room? Look to the left of it and then down.

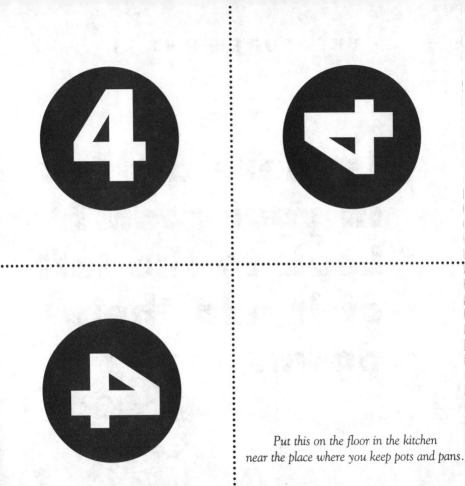

Put this on the floor in the kitchen near the place where you keep pots and pans.

Outstanding! Please come get your sticker.

MATCH IT!

clock

block

dock

lock

knock

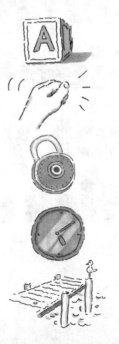

Put this to the left of and below the clock in your child's room.

Hey there
Today is a treasure hunt day. There are four clues.

1. Go to the bathroom and look near the sink.

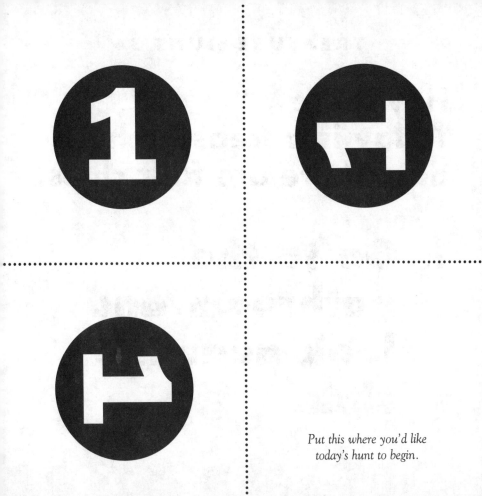

*Put this where you'd like
today's hunt to begin.*

2. Where do you eat breakfast? Look under your chair.

Put this near the sink in the bathroom.

3. Is there a pot or pan near the kitchen sink that is hiding a clue?

Put this under the chair
where your child eats breakfast.

4. Where are your blocks? Look there.

Put this in or under a pot or pan near the kitchen sink.

Very, very good! Come get your sticker, please.

MATCH IT!

block

blimp

blanket

blow

blink

Put this with your child's blocks.

Howdy
Today is a treasure hunt
day. There are four clues.

**1. Where do
we keep the
spoons, forks,
and knives?**

Put this where you'd like today's hunt to begin.

2. Please look on the freezer door.

Put this with your silverware.

3. Look to the right of the clock near my bed.

Attach this to the freezer door.

4. **You will find the last clue behind my bedroom door.**

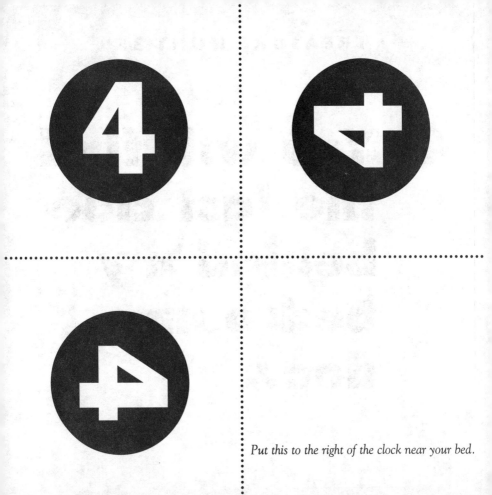

Put this to the right of the clock near your bed.

Excellent! Come ask me for your sticker.

MATCH IT!

BONUS GAME

clock

cloud

clip

clothes

clap

Put this behind your bedroom door.

Hi
Today is a treasure hunt day. There are four clues.

1. If you spill orange juice, you need to clean it up. Look under the sponge.

Put this where you'd like today's hunt to begin.

2. **If you go to the window in your room, turn left and look down, you will find a clue.**

Put this under the kitchen sponge.

3. Look on the TV page of the newspaper.

Put this to the left of and down from the window in your child's room.

4. When it is time to put away your toys, where do they go?

Put this on the last page of the newspaper.

Wonderful job! Come get your sticker.

MATCH IT!

spoon

splash

spill

spaghetti

sponge

Put this where you keep your child's toys.

**Good morning
Today is a treasure hunt
day. There are four clues.**

**1. In your room,
please look
near one of
your favorite
toys.**

Put this where you'd like today's hunt to begin.

2. What do we use to sweep the floor?

Put this near one of your child's favorite toys in his or her room.

3. There is a clue taped to the bottom of a chair in your room.

Put this near the broom.

4. Where do we keep eggs? Look there for today's last clue.

*Tape this to the bottom of a chair
in your child's room.*

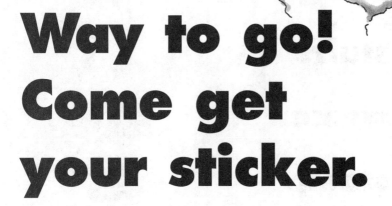

Way to go!
Come get
your sticker.

MATCH IT!

stump

stairs

sticker

stamp

star

Put this where you keep eggs.

Hello there
I hope you are having fun
with the treasure hunts.
There are four clues today.

1. Where do you watch movies or cartoons? Look on top of the television.

Put this where you'd like today's hunt to begin.

2. To make a sandwich or French toast, you need bread. Where do we keep it?

Put this on top of the TV.

3. **Please open the newspaper to the last page. You will find the next clue there.**

Put this where you keep bread.

4. **When you want to listen to music, you turn on this machine.**

Put this on the TV page of the newspaper.

Wonderful!
Come get
your
sticker.

MATCH IT!

brush

bridge

broom

bread

broccoli

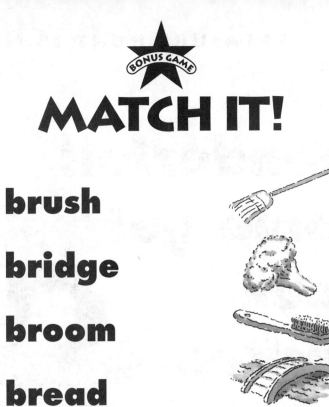

Put this next to the machine (radio, tape or CD player, etc.) that your child most often uses to listen to music.

Hi
Welcome to the treasure hunt.
There are four clues.

1. Can you find a book that we read together yesterday or the day before?

Put this where you'd like today's hunt to begin.

2. Where do we keep a yellow fruit?

Put this in a book that you and your child read together yesterday or the day before.

3. Take a look at what is taped inside the closet door in my room.

Put this where you keep bananas, lemons, or other yellow fruit.

4. Look in the drawer where you keep your underwear.

Tape this to the inside of your closet door.

If you have time, "personalize" the first clue by writing your child's name in the blank space after the greeting. (Children love this personalization, and one of the first words they learn to recognize is their own name.)

Hello *Chris !*

Put the first clue in a place where your child is sure to see it. Even better, tell your child beforehand that she will be doing a treasure hunt and that she should expect to find the first clue in a specific place.

Hide the other clues. (They are numbered on the back. Plus, for your conveniece—or if you're trying to do this before you've had your morning coffee—the reverse side of each clue tells you exactly where to hide it.)

Finally, be ready to help your child when she asks for it. (More on this later.) And have that sticker ready when she finds the last clue!

SOME PERSONAL SUGGESTIONS ABOUT HOW TO PLAY

Everyone likes to do things slightly differently, and no two homes are exactly alike. You will decide how the treasure hunts work best for you and your child. But we want to share these suggestions based on our personal experiences.

Play early and play often. Hide the clues after your child goes to bed, and have the first clue waiting for him when he gets to the breakfast table. The combination of regularity and predictability reinforces the experience. For Peter, it was something he looked forward to doing on his own each morning, and it had the added benefit of giving us a few more minutes of free time during the morning routine.

This said, kids don't have to play the quiz every day! Play the treasure hunt when it feels right for you and your child.

Personalize and customize the clues if you have time. Obviously, when I first wrote the clues, each was written for Peter and reflected

the particular layout of our home. For this book, we've tried to craft clues that are appropriate for most any home. Realistically, however, not every clue will fit perfectly in every home. So don't hesi-tate to change a word, a location, or a description to reflect your home or your child's preferences.

Occassionally, a clue will say something like, "Look under the chair near the window." Your home may have two chairs near a window, and it is perfectly logical for your child to look under the one without the clue. Anticipating that, we've included a few extra clues that say

No, not this one, try another.

Obviously, you should feel free to make as many more of the "No, not this one" clues as appropriate for your home. Similarly, you may want to customize clues by adding descriptive words or colors.

For example, you might write in the word "green" before "chair," or include the name for a favorite stuffed animal.

Hide clues well, but not too well. You don't want clues to be so obvious that your child can find them even without reading them. But we also found that hiding clues too well could be discouraging. For us, folding them in quarters and then hiding them just out of plain sight—with a little tape if necessary—worked well. Follow your child's lead; she'll let you know if something is too hard or too easy!

THE "RULES"

Every game has rules. *Learn-to-Read-Treasure Hunts* has fewer and simpler rules than most.

Rule #1: Keep it fun. Don't nag your kid; don't get disappointed when he doesn't "get" something. Laugh. Share the joy of discovery.

Rule #2: Be flexible. If your child wants fewer questions, that's OK. If she wants to try questions that are tougher than you think she can handle, let her try.

Rule #3: Help your child. Your child will probably find some clues too tough, some words unfamiliar. Encourage him to guess. (Remember, guessing is a legitimate "decoding" strategy.) Or just tell him! In general, give help when it's asked for; you are trying to build self-confidence and risk taking, not just basic skills.

Rule #4: Remember Rule #1.

MORE ON HELPING YOUR CHILD

Don't be surprised or disappointed, but at some point your child is not going to be able to read a word or be able to figure out a clue. Help her!

When your child asks you for help with a word, don't immediately say, "Sound it out." (Most parents are inclined to do

just that, forgetting their own frustration and fury when their own parents said that to them.)

Instead, you might ask her if she knows the first letter and what sound that makes. You should then encourage her to guess! But be sure to give the help requested.

Try other hints: "What rhymes with boat?" Or, "Think of a piece of clothing." Or, "It's red and you wear it."

You don't need to get too creative. Just remember that you are dealing with a young person who, while perhaps sophisticated in many ways, is acquiring a skill more formidable—and formal—than most mastered so far. Reading is a major passage into the adult world.

"Sight" Words

Some words, like "look," "where," "on," even "the," are not easily sounded out. Many children simply memorize them; they become "sight" words. It is important for you to recognize that these "easy"

words can indeed be quite difficult for a new reader. So if your child doesn't recognize them the first few times he sees them in a clue, it is often best to simply tell him the word. He'll memorize it soon enough.

When Your Child Guesses Wrong

Some children will see the picture of the coat and immediately guess "jacket." In a technical sense, they are wrong; the correct word is "coat." But they are also quite correct in decoding the meaning of the sentence!

Your response should be, "Great job!" And then you should point out the letter "C" and the correct word, "coat." But the praise should come before—and with more emphasis than—the correction. The next time your child sees the clue—with or without the drawing of the jacket, uh, I mean coat—the odds are he will identify it as a coat.

17

If your child gets stuck on a word, encourage him by reminding him that he saw that very word in a clue just a few days or weeks ago. Don't be reticent to supply hints!

Word Difficulty

The clues are relatively simple at the beginning and get progressively more difficult each week. Although the words were chosen with the guidance of reading specialists, no two children respond in exactly the same way to the same words.

It is important to remember that "difficulty" is a relative term. Children progress at individual rates with varying degrees of comfort with particular types of words. Some kids have trouble with certain types of words, while others are challenged by completely different sets. Don't worry if your child has trouble with an "easy" word.

Pictures

For the first few weeks, every clue is accompanied by a picture. This

helps kids decode the meaning. As each week passes—and your child's reading skills improve—there are fewer and fewer pictures. By week six, the pictures are few and far between.

The combination of picture-assisted decoding and repetition is a key to building the young reader's skills and confidence.

Feel free to adapt or cross out the pictures, or to add new pictures to the clues. The illustrations are designed to be a tool, not a trap or crutch.

The "Right" Age

All children learn to read a bit differently, at different rates, and at different ages. The words and sentences in the *Learn-to-Read Treasure Hunts* are geared to emerging readers. It is important to understand that the "right age" for this reading level can easily span two years. For many kids—but certainly not for all, or even a majority—reading starts to "click" some time in the middle of first

grade. But some kids will be ready as early as kindergarten and others will be reluctant to try it in second grade. Children are, however, tested at the end of third grade and are expected to be reading at grade level.

Listening to Your Child

You will quickly get feedback from your child about the right pace for him to proceed with the treasure hunt. **Don't be impatient to move your child too quickly to harder clues.**

If your child finds the hunt too hard when you first try it—or if the progression of clues moves too quickly—put it away for several weeks or even months. You want to associate reading with fun and not set it up as a chore or unpleasant experience.

The key is not to let frustration—yours principally—overwhelm your child's willingness to take risks. You are trying to encourage your child and to help her build the self-confidence she

needs to want to sound out words. As your child begins to develop skills—and confidence—it is important for her to see you taking joy in her progress as well.

The Bottom Line
Help *sooner*, rather than later.

REWARDS

At the back of this book is a set of stickers. (The original idea to include stickers was Peter's.) We recommend that you give your child one sticker for every trea-sure hunt he completes. This gives him a tangible, immediate—but not excessive—reward for com-pleting a challenging task.

Many parents have found it effective to allow their child to trade a certain number of stickers—usually a week's worth of five—for a special treat, for example, a movie, an ice cream cone, or a pizza party.

Bribery vs. Encouragement

Experts simply do not agree on when prizes—intended as rewards and encouragement—become bribes. It's different for every child and family.

Some parents and teachers think that prizes set a bad precedent, and will only lead to ever-escalating rewards for something the child should do anyway—indeed should want to do. Others argue that more than simple encouragement is necessary for some children. And if a small toy or modest amount of money gets the child over the hurdles of learning to read, it is no big deal.

Obviously it is up to each individual parent to make this decision. One piece of advice: the more modest you keep the prize, the easier it is to "ratchet up" the rewards later for more difficult work.

We found that giving Peter one or two super-hero trading cards for completing a treasure hunt was more effective than rewarding him with a whole pack. Similarly, giving him a dime for a tough

question answered correctly was more effective than a dollar—it kept the exercise in perspective. We also used special trips to the zoo, aquarium, McDonalds. They all worked.

A BIT OF PERSPECTIVE:
HOW SCHOOLS TEACH READING

As a parent you will hear teachers, principals, reading specialists, and media commentators talk about different approaches to teaching reading. Some of the buzz words bandied about include:

- Core and supplemental programs
- Basal programs
- Phonics
- Whole language

What do these mean? Which does your child's school use? Which should it use? And which approach is best for your child?

Core and Supplemental

The first set of buzz words you should know are *core* and *supplemental*. Core simply refers to the basic reading program used by the school. Typically an entire district—or even state—will "adopt" a particular approach to reading, and that is referred to as the core reading program.

Supplemental reading materials simply refer to all other books, magazines, and reading tools—other than the core texts—in the individual classrooms.

Basal Programs

From about 1930 until 1960, most children in the United States were taught to read by what is known as the basal reading method. This method uses a look-and-say, or whole-word-memorization, approach. Many schools today still use basal readers to a certain extent.

The basal method presents children with a number of whole

words that need to be memorized. As a small vocabulary of sight words is accumulated, the child is taught to notice certain beginning letters and their corresponding sounds. The child is then taught to apply these phonic elements to new words encountered. But rarely is there an emphasis on teaching the phonic sounds made by individual letters, at least not in the beginning.

The pace of basal readers is quite slow, with new sight words introduced very gradually, often one per page. The words are thereafter repeated, and meaning is stressed. When children have "mastered" a level of words, they move on to the next level.

Basal programs typically involve a combination of "leveled readers," drill-and-practice worksheets, literature, and some phonics.

If you remember, "Run, Dick, run. See Dick run," you are recalling your own exposure to a basal system.

Phonics

Phonics—the predictable sounds that letters and combinations of letters make—introduces kids to the symbol-sound relationship of letters. There are some 40 to 50 different letter combinations, and children learn to decode a wide range of words as they learn the rules that apply to the different combinations.

Today phonics instruction is perhaps the most hotly contested issue among educators. The vast majority of schools do use phonics, to one degree or another, to teach reading. What makes phonics such an emotional and debated issue is the *extent* to which it is used.

Until the introduction of basal systems, phonics dominated reading instruction. Indeed, it is still used in many countries around the world. Thus the question so many educators and parents raise is, "If phonics worked here in the United States for so many years, is still used so extensively abroad, and our kids' reading scores continue to fall, why aren't we using phonics again?"

Good question. Indeed there is a strong "traditional" movement in the country to go back to phonics as the core method to teach reading. In part, this is a reaction to the "whole language" approach to teaching reading that has dominated the education establishment for the last ten or so years.

There are three pieces to the argument against focusing too heavily on phonics:

First, English, unlike most other foreign languages, has almost as many exceptions to phonetic rules as rules themselves.

Second, phonics alone—without counterbalancing literature—can be very dry and repetitious. Reading should be fun, joyful.

Third, phonics without context and meaning does not promote comprehension. To simply have the ability to sound out a word without a sense of what it means does not promote literacy; it simply builds the ability to sound out words.

Phonics proponents, however, justifiably point to im-

proved test scores among children whose reading instruction has been phonics-heavy.

Whole Language

About ten years ago, a new phrase emerged on the learning-to-read scene: whole language. As a concept or system it wasn't radically new—it had been in use and evolving for some time—but it was suddenly achieving critical mass as an accepted, formal approach.

The core philosophy of whole language is quite simple: children learn best when there is context to what they are learning, when it relates to their life.

All of us read to get meaning: we read a newspaper to learn about events of the day; we read a novel for the pleasure of the story; we read a cookbook in order to attempt a recipe.

28

Children need to get meaning as well. And while very young children do not yet have many tools to decode the written words around them, they are immersed in a language-rich environment. They hear parents, siblings, friends, other adults talk. They see cereal boxes and store signs and newspapers on a daily basis. And they want to make sense of the words and writing all around them.

The whole language approach to reading is based on the connection between children's desire to get meaning and their daily experiences. It is not building reading skills through drills such as: "See Dick run. See Jane run. See Spot run to Dick and Jane."

Rather, whole language builds on experiences that are real for the child: his friends' names, daily routine, compelling stories.

Whole language proponents argue that children learn best when there is context and meaning, and that tools such as phonics are most effective when they are incorporated somewhat later into the reading mix.

What Is the Best System to Teach Reading?

That depends on your child's personal strengths, weaknesses, and interests. But if there were a vote held among school administrators, reading experts, and teachers, it would probably degenerate into a screaming match.

If you ask back-to-basics advocates, phonics would be the hands-down winner. If you ask teachers, a majority would probably argue for a whole language approach supported by some phonics. And among school administrators, who are under the most pressure to deliver higher test scores, a comprehensive program of phonics and literature would probably win.

The key is to make sure your child is exposed to each system. In that way you can see for yourself which set of tools works for your kid.

30

WHY THE HUNTS WORK WITH ANY SCHOOL-BASED SYSTEM

Learn-to-Read Treasure Hunts works with any school-based program. Why? For three reasons:

It conveys real meaning. Even the simplest clues are "real"—they lead the child to concrete places around the home and trigger immediate reinforcement.

It supports different "decoding" strategies. Some children learn to read by "sounding out" words. Other kids memorize the "picture" of the word. And still others prefer to guess at words in the context of the whole sentence. The game supports whatever combination of decoding strategies your child uses. It allows kids to build on their strengths, while developing confidence to try other methods.

It reinforces phonics. The *Match It!* phonics games are designed to complement the word choices in that day's clues. They are not simply exercises in a vacuum.

A Sense of Accomplishment Plus Fun

Learning to read is hard work. But the sense of accomplishment a child derives from decoding a clue is very special. It can be made even more special when the experience itself is fun. (And one should never underestimate the importance—or power—of fun!) *Learn-to-Read Treasure Hunts* combines all these elements.

A NOTE FROM PETER COHEN, AGE 10

Hi. My name is Peter Cohen, the co-writer of this book, and I hope you like it. I'm 10 years old, and I started this book when I was 7. In the beginning, I helped my dad by telling him what words to use; which words were too easy and which were too hard. I suggested good places to hide clues.

32

Learning how to read at first was pretty hard, but when I got the hang of it with the treasure hunts, it was really fun. The hardest part about learning how to read was sounding out the words. That's because a lot of words are spelled a lot differently than they sound. The treasure hunts helped because I got used to the words that were repeated, and then moved on to new words.

I love treasure hunts because they are something to look forward to when you are learning. When you're really young it makes you feel proud to be able to read a whole treasure hunt.

My advice to kids is: don't be scared; it's only a game. If you mess up, just go to your parents and ask for help with a word. After a few times, you'll know it by heart. To parents I want to say: if your kids mess up, don't get mad at them. Tell them it is not a test, but a fun game.

I hope all the kids who use this—including my little brother, Jacob—have a good time and feel proud.

PLEASE LET US KNOW
WHAT YOU THINK

We hope you find these exercises as enjoyable and satisfying—for both parent and child—as we have. A bit of advice I'll give one last time: keep it fun! If you are anxious about your child's progress, it will thwart her progress—and her joy in reading.

So, have fun, good hunting, and good reading!

If you have any questions, comments, or suggests, e-mail us at SteveCBald@AOL.com. We very much want to hear from you and will get back to you as soon as possible.

And in advance, thanks for taking the time to share your thoughts.

Hello
Today is a treasure hunt
day. There are 3 clues.

1. Look under
a pan.

*Put this where you'd like
today's hunt to begin.*

2. Look under your bed.

Put this under a pan.

3. Look under the bath mat.

Put this under your child's bed.

Great.
You did it!
Come get
your sticker.

AWESOME!

★ BONUS GAME

MATCH IT!

apple

bat

cap

pan

sad

Put this under a bath mat.

Hi
Today is a treasure hunt day. There are 3 clues.

1. Look under a table.

*Put this where you'd like
today's hunt to begin.*

No, not this one. Try another table.

*Use this clue if there are two tables that
you think your child would likely look under.
Put this under one of them.*

2. Look on top of a TV.

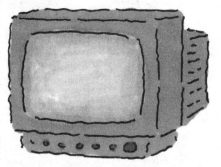

Put this under a table.

3. Look near a mop.

Put this on top of a TV.

Way to go! Come get your sticker.

BONUS GAME

MATCH IT!

mop

doll

frog

pot

sock

Put this near a mop.

Hello
Today is a treasure hunt
day. There are 3 clues.

1. Look next to the bathtub.

Put this where you'd like today's hunt to begin.

2. **Where do we keep milk? Go there.**

Put this next to the bathtub.

3. Look next to your bed.

Put this in the refrigerator near or under the milk.

Great job! Come get your sticker.

MATCH IT!

hen

ten

bed

egg

leg

Put this next to your child's bed.

TREASURE HUNT 4

Hello
Today is a treasure hunt day. There are 3 clues.

1. Look under a cup.

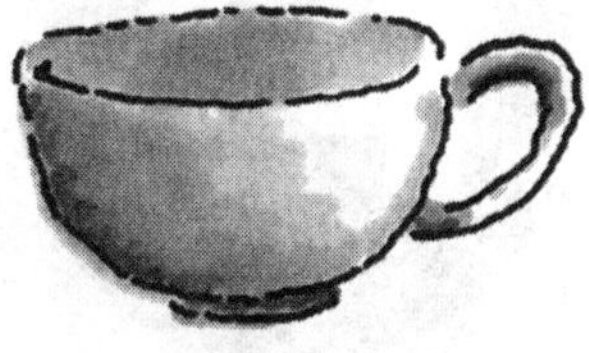

*Put this where you'd like
today's hunt to begin.*

2. Find a pen.

Put this under a cup.

3. Look under the table where we eat.

*Put this where your child
would look for a pen.*

Super!
Come get
your sticker.

MATCH IT!

jet

net

bell

pen

tent

Put this under the table where your child eats.

Hi there
Today is a treasure hunt day. There are 3 clues.

1. Look behind the door to your room.

Put this where you'd like today's hunt to begin.

2. Your next clue is under the couch.

Put this behind the door to your child's room.

3. Where is the toilet? Go there.

Put this under the couch.

Excellent! Come get your sticker.

MATCH IT!

couch

crouch

mouse

cloud

mouth

Put this near the toilet.

Hello again
Today is a treasure hunt
day. There are 3 clues.

1. Look near the bathtub.

*Put this where you'd like
today's hunt to begin.*

2. What is behind the chair nearest to the TV?

Put this near the bathtub.

3. Take a peek under your bed.

*Put this behind the chair
nearest to the TV.*

Fantastic! Come get your sticker.

AWESOME!

MATCH IT!

leg

bed

neck

pen

egg

Put this under your child's bed.

Good morning
Today is a treasure hunt
day. There are 3 clues.

1. Where do we keep the spoons?

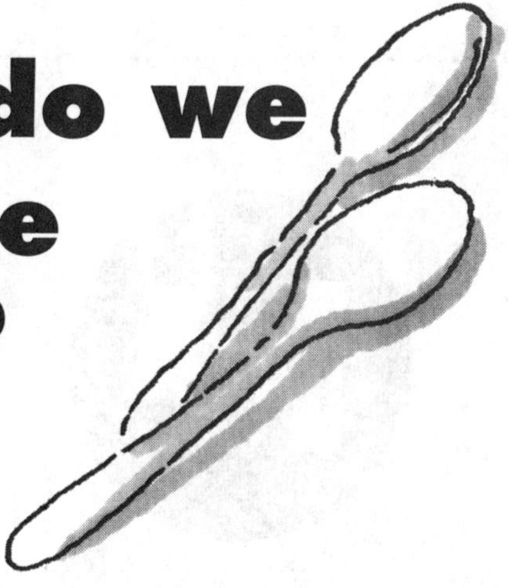

Put this where you'd like today's hunt to begin.

2. Look near a stuffed animal.

Put this with the spoons.

3. Where do we wash dishes? Go to that sink.

Put this near a stuffed animal.

Great!
Come get
your sticker.

MATCH IT!

dish

ship

sink

fist

hill

Put this next to the kitchen sink.

Hello
Today is a treasure hunt day. There are 3 clues.

1. Look near the VCR.

Put this where you'd like today's hunt to begin.

2. There is a book near your bed. Look in it.

Put this near the VCR.

3. You will find your last clue near the bathtub.

Put this in a book near your child's bed.

Wonderful!
Come get
your sticker.

MATCH IT!

bug

bag

book

bed

bathtub

Put this near the bathtub.

Hi
Today is a treasure hunt day. There are 3 clues.

1. Look under the newspaper.

*Put this where you'd like
today's hunt to begin.*

2. Look behind the milk.

Put this under the newspaper.

3. Check under your pillow.

Put this in the refrigerator behind the milk.

Great!
Come get
your sticker.

MATCH IT!

pig

sticker

milk

lips

pillow

Put this under your child's pillow.

Good morning
Today is a treasure hunt
day. There are 3 clues.

1. Where do you
keep your
toothbrush?
Go there.

*Put this where you'd like
today's hunt to begin.*

2. Look near the clock in my room.

Put this near your child's toothbrush.

3. Go to the kitchen and look on the floor near the refrigerator.

Put this near the clock in your room.

Excellent reading! Come get your sticker.

MATCH IT!

bathtub

bed

sink

shoe

refrigerator

Put this on the floor near the refrigerator.

Good morning
Today is a treasure hunt
day. There are 3 clues.

1. Where do
we keep the
broom?

Put this where you'd like today's hunt to begin.

2. Is there a light switch in my bedroom? Go to it and look down.

Put this next to your broom.

3. Look under a glass or a cup.

Put this on the floor below the light switch in your room.

MATCH IT!

bus

rug

cup

butter

sun

Put this under a glass or a cup.

Hello
Today is a treasure hunt day. There are 3 clues.

1. Look under today's newspaper.

Put this where you'd like today's hunt to begin.

2. Find your coat and look in a pocket.

Put this under today's newspaper.

3. There is a pan near the kitchen sink. Look under the pan.

Put this in your child's coat pocket.

Excellent! Come get your sticker.

MATCH IT!

cap

cup

kite

key

coat

Put this under a pan next to the kitchen sink.

Hi there
Today is a treasure hunt
day. There are 3 clues.

1. Look near a plant or flowers.

*Put this where you'd like
today's hunt to begin.*

2. Where do we keep crayons or markers?

Put this near a plant or flowers.

3. From your bedroom window, you can see the sky and the next clue.

Put this near the crayons or markers.

Way to go! Come get your sticker.

MATCH IT!

window

web

witch

wheel

walrus

**Hey there
Today is a treasure hunt
day. There are 3 clues.**

**1. Look behind a
   lamp in the
   living room.**

Put this where you'd like today's hunt to begin.

2. Is there a clue behind a cup or a glass in the kitchen?

Put this behind a lamp in the living room.

3. Look behind a picture of you or me.

Put this under a cup or glass in the kitchen.

Good work! Come get your sticker.

MATCH IT!

cat

candy

cup

can

card

Put this behind a picture of you and/or your child.

**Welcome back
Today is a treasure hunt
day. There are 3 clues.**

**1. Look behind
a clock in
my room.**

Put this where you'd like today's hunt to begin.

2. You will find the next clue near a living room window.

Put this behind a clock in your room.

3. The next clue is under a plate in the kitchen.

Put this near a window in the living room.

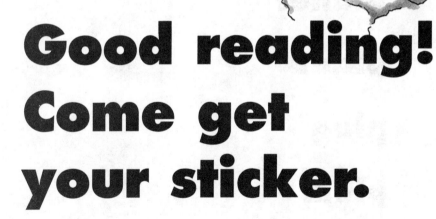

Good reading! Come get your sticker.

MATCH IT!

planet

plant

plug

plum

plate

Put this under a plate in the kitchen.

Hello again
Today is a treasure hunt day. There are 3 clues.

1. Go to the bathroom and find the clue near the sink.

Put this where you'd like today's hunt to begin.

2. Look under the chairs at the table where you eat.

Put this near the bathroom sink.

3. Where do we keep your socks?

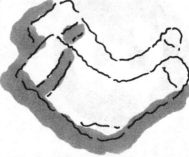

*Put this under a chair at the table
where your child eats.*

Outstanding! Come get your sticker.

★ BONUS GAME
MATCH IT!

sock

rock

neck

stick

backpack

Put this where you keep your child's socks.

Hey there
Today is a treasure hunt
day. There are 3 clues.

1. Where do we keep the spoons?

Put this where you'd like today's hunt to begin.

2. Look near the toothpaste and your toothbrush.

Put this with your spoons.

3. Look behind my bedroom door.

Put this near your child's toothbrush.

You are a great reader! Come get your sticker.

MATCH IT!

duck

lock

back

truck

sticker

Put this behind your bedroom door.

TREASURE HUNT 18

Hello
Today is a treasure hunt day. There are 3 clues.

1. Look behind your bath towel.

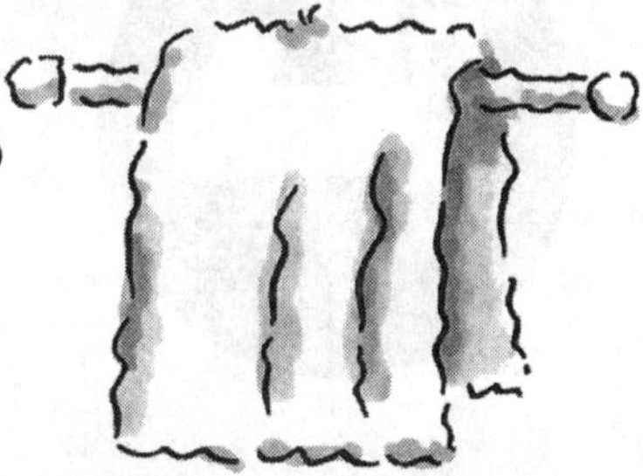

Put this where you'd like today's hunt to begin.

2. Where do we keep milk? Look there.

Put this behind your child's bath towel.

3. Look in a cup next to the kitchen sink.

Put this in the refrigerator near the milk.

Wonderful! Come get your sticker.

MATCH IT!

owl

shower

flower

cow

towel

Put this in a cup next to the kitchen sink.

Hello
Today is a treasure hunt day. There are 3 clues.

1. Where do we keep the butter and eggs?

Put this where you'd like today's hunt to begin.

2. Look on page 2 of today's newspaper.

Put this in the refrigerator, near the butter and/or eggs.

3. Look under a pillow on the couch.

Put this on page 2 of today's newspaper.

Fantastic! Come get your sticker.

MATCH IT!

butter

suds

puppy

truck

sun

Put this under a pillow on the couch.

Hi
Today is a treasure hunt
day. There are 3 clues.

1. In the
   bathroom,
   look near the
   toothpaste.

Put this where you'd like today's hunt to begin.

2. Where do we keep the juice? Look there.

Put this near the toothpaste in the bathroom.

3. Look under the chair near the desk.

Put this in the refrigerator near the juice.

Perfect! Come get your sticker.

MATCH IT!

ski

desk

mask

tusk

waste paper basket

Put this under the chair near the desk.

Hello again
Today is a treasure hunt day. There are 3 clues.

1. Look near a lamp on a table in the living room.

*Put this where you'd like
today's hunt to begin.*

2. Where would you find an apple?

Put this near a lamp on a table in the living room.

3. Take a peek at the soap in the bathtub.

Put this where you keep apples.

Super! Come get your sticker.

MATCH IT!

stamp

stump

bump

lamp

ramp

Put this next to the soap in the bathtub.

**Howdy
Today is a treasure hunt
day. There are 3 clues.**

1. Look under the telephone.

Put this where you'd like today's hunt to begin.

2. **There is a pot on the kitchen counter. Look under it.**

Put this under a telephone.

3. Do we have a desk? Check under it.

Put this under a pot on the kitchen counter.

Great. You are a winner! Please come get your sticker.

MATCH IT!

desk

mask

belt

nest

lamp

Put this under a desk.

**Good morning
Today is a treasure hunt
day. There are 3 clues.**

**1. Look in a
book near
my bed.**

Put this where you'd like today's hunt to begin.

2. Check out page 4 of the newspaper.

Put this in a book near your bed.

3. Where do we keep the Band-Aids?

Put this on page 4 of the newspaper.

Fantastic! Come get your sticker.

MATCH IT!

BONUS GAME

hand

candy

pond

wand

Band-Aid

Put this near where you keep the Band-Aids.

Hi
Today is a treasure hunt day. There are 3 clues.

1. Look under the chair where I like to read.

*Put this where you'd like
today's hunt to begin.*

2. Where do we eat breakfast? Look under the table.

Put this under the chair where you like to read.

3. Where do we keep the broom or mop?

*Put this under the table
where your child eats breakfast.*

Good thinking! Come get your sticker.

MATCH IT!

broom

goose

moose

tooth

boot

Put this where you keep your broom or mop.

Hey there
Today is a treasure hunt
day. There are 3 clues.

1. Look behind the door to your bedroom.

Put this where you'd like today's hunt to begin.

2. Try looking under a pillow on the couch.

*Put this behind the door
to your child's bedroom.*

3. Where do we keep forks?

Put this under a pillow on the couch.

Excellent!
Come get
your sticker.

MATCH IT!

grouch

ouch

couch

cloud

round

Hello
Today is a treasure hunt
day. There are 3 clues.

1. Take a look on
   the floor near
   the bathtub.

*Put this where you'd like
today's hunt to begin.*

2. **What room is the sofa in? Go to that room and look under a chair.**

Put this on the floor near the bathtub.

3. Look under the yellow telephone book.

*Put this under a chair in the room
that contains the sofa.*

Great! Come get your sticker.

MATCH IT!

tub

duck

bubble

butter

stump

Put this under the Yellow Pages.

Good morning
Today is a treasure hunt
day. There are 3 clues.

1. Go behind the
door in your
bedroom and
look down,
then up.

Put this where you'd like today's hunt to begin.

2. Where do we hang our coats and jackets? Look in a pocket.

Tape this behind your child's bedroom door, above eye level.

3. Where do we keep your shirts? Look under the one on the bottom.

Put this in a coat or jacket pocket.

Terrific job! Come get your sticker.

★ BONUS GAME

MATCH IT!

lung

hanger

lightning

ring

king

Put this where you keep your child's shirts, under the shirt on the bottom.

THE LAST GAME!

Unscramble these words.

T G E R A

O B J

Congratulations! You have finished the treasure hunt and become a great reader.

*Put this where you keep
a blue crayon or marker.*

4. **For your last clue, look in the coldest spot in the house. (Hint: It is not a room.)**

Put this behind a photograph of your child.

3. **To draw pictures, we need crayons or markers. Find a blue one.**

Put this in the left shoe of a pair your child wears to play outside.

2. For your next clue, find a photograph of yourself and look behind it.

*Put this where you'd like
today's hunt to begin.*

Hey there
Today is the last treasure hunt day. There are four clues.

1. What shoes do you wear when you want to play games outside? Look in the left one.

MATCH IT!

cake

flake

rake

shake

awake

Wonderful!
Come get
your sticker.

Put this on your child's bed.

4. **Soap and shampoo both start with the same letter. Do you wear anything that starts with the same letter? Look where you keep them for your next clue. (Hint: They have sleeves, and you wear them to keep extra warm.)**

Put this on page 16 of a book you and your child read yesterday or the day before.

3. **What is the opposite of "awake"? Where do you do this? Look there.**

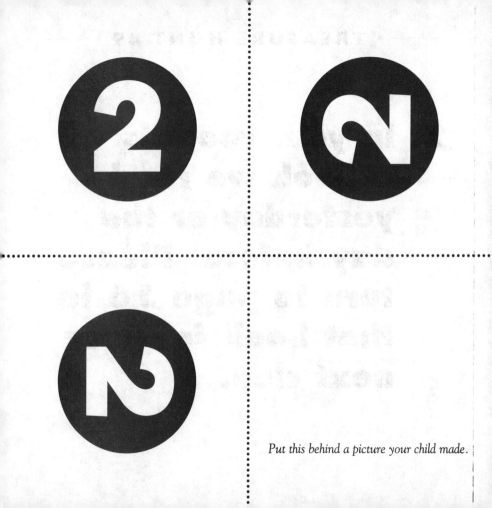

Put this behind a picture your child made.

2. **In your room is a book we read yesterday or the day before. Please turn to page 16 in that book for your next clue.**

*Put this where you'd like
today's hunt to begin.*

Hello
Today is a treasure hunt
day. There are four clues.

1. **The first clue is hidden behind a picture you made.**

★ MATCH IT!

queen

quack

quarter

quilt

question mark

Put this on the weather map page of the newspaper.

Way to go! Come get your sticker, but first answer this question: Can you find the word "cloudy" on this page of the newspaper?

Put this on the kitchen counter near where you would let pots dry.

3. Please open the newspaper to the weather map. You will find your next clue there.

Put this on the right side of your bottom dresser drawer.

2. After we wash pots and pans, sometimes we let them dry on the kitchen counter. Look there for your next clue.

*Put this where you'd like
today's hunt to begin.*

Hello
Today is a treasure hunt day.
There are three clues.

1. Please go to my bedroom. Look for the next clue on the right side of the bottom drawer of my dresser.

BONUS GAME

MATCH IT!

face

fireplace

laces

ace

braces

Put this in the sports section of the newspaper next to a story with a picture of someone playing baseball, football, or basketball.

Great job! Come get your sticker. But first, can you tell me the name of a sports team that won last night?

Put this with your child's socks.

3. Look in the newspaper. Can you find a story with a picture of someone playing baseball, football, or basketball?

Put this inside one of your child's books that features either a rabbit or a dinosaur.

2. The next clue is hiding with something that goes on your feet. (Hint: It doesn't have laces.)

Put this where you'd like today's hunt to begin.

Hi
Today is a treasure hunt day.
There are three clues.

1. In your room, find
   a book that has a
   picture of rabbit or
   a dinosaur. Look
   inside that book for
   your next clue.

MATCH IT!

lunch box

punch

pinch

bench

branch

Put this where you keep the napkins.

Super! Come get your sticker.

Put this under a table that's next to a chair in the living room.

3. Think about where we make breakfast, lunch, and dinner. Where do we keep napkins?

Put this next to the radio.

2. There is a table next to a chair in the living room. Look under it.

Put this where you'd like today's hunt to begin.

Hey there
Today is a treasure hunt day.
There are three clues.

1. **Some people use the
   r _ _ _ _ to listen to
   music. Other people
   use it to listen to
   the news. A clue is
   hidden next to it.**

MATCH IT!

church

cheese

cherry

chicken

chin

Put this next to the milk in the refrigerator.

Terrific! Come get your sticker, please.

Put this on page 20 of a book you like to read and put the book in the living room.

4. You will find the last clue in a cold place. It is near a drink that cows make.

Put this under your child's bath towel.

3. **In the living room, you will find a book that I like to read. Look for your next clue on page 20.**

Put this in one of your shoes in your closet.

2. **Go to the room where you take your bath. Can you find the clue hidden under your towel?**

Put this where you'd like today's hunt to begin.

Hello
Today is a treasure hunt day.
There are four clues.

1. There is a clue in my closet. To find it, look in one of my shoes.

MATCH IT!

whistle

whale

whisper

wheel

whisker

Put this under the biggest chair in the living room.

Nice job! Please see me for your sticker.

Put this near the kitchen sink.

3. Which is the biggest chair in the living room? Take a look under it.

Tape this to the bottom of a toy with wheels in your child's room.

2. Before we cook vegetables like green beans or broccoli, we wash them. Where do we do that?

Put this where you'd like today's hunt to begin.

Hi
Today is a treasure hunt day.
There are three clues.

1. There is a toy with wheels in your room. Lift it and see what is taped to the bottom.

MATCH IT!

truck

trumpet

train

traffic light

trash can

Put this in the refrigerator.

That was great reading! Come get your sticker.

Put this under the chair that is closest to the sofa in the living room.

3. If you want to make pancakes, you need to mix flour, eggs, and milk in a bowl. The flour, eggs, and milk are called ingredients. Where would you find eggs and milk?

Put this behind the trash can in the kitchen.

2. Look under the chair that is closest to the sofa in the living room.

Put this where you'd like today's hunt to begin.

Good morning
Today is a treasure hunt
day. There are three clues.

1. You will find
the next clue if
you look behind
the trash can
in the kitchen.

MATCH IT!

green bean

grasshopper

grapes

grin

grade

Put this to the right of and below the telephone nearest to the alarm clock or clock radio.

Superb!
Would you like a
sticker? Please
come tell
me how
old you are.

Put this near an alarm clock or clock radio

3. Please go to the nearest telephone, then turn right and look down.

Put this in the refrigerator.

2. **Sometimes it's hard to wake up in the morning, so we use this clock to help.**

*Put this where you'd like
today's hunt to begin.*

Hello
Today is a treasure hunt day.
There are three clues.

1. Green beans and grapes are kept cold here.

MATCH IT!

French fry

frog

freezer

Frankenstein

fruit

Put this on the last page of the Yellow Pages.

**Super!
To get your
sticker, come
see me and say the
secret password:
frog.**

*Put this next to or under
a piece of fruit in the refrigerator.*

3. **Please open the yellow telephone book to the last page.**

Put this behind a photograph of your child.

2. Find a piece of fruit that we keep in the refrigerator.

MATCH IT!

BONUS GAME

drum

drip

dress

drawer

dragon

Put this in your child's underwear drawer.

Well done! Come get your sticker.